Life Science Quick Starts

Author: Gary Raham
Editor: Mary Dieterich
Proofreaders: Margaret Brown and Cindy Neisen

COPYRIGHT © 2018 Mark Twain Media, Inc.

ISBN 978-1-62223-693-0

Printing No. CD-405016

Mark Twain Media, Inc., Publishers
Distributed by Carson-Dellosa Publishing LLC

Visit www.carsondellosa.com

Table of Contents

Introduction to the Teacher

Scientific investigation uses skills in observation, reading, critical thinking, research, manipulation, math, and learning how to ask questions that can be answered through experimentation. Students need practice in using these skills to investigate the living world around them in a systematic way.

This book provides quick warm-up activities that will exercise these skills in six broad categories: the diversity of life, energy flow in living communities (ecosystems), the form and operation of the human body, descent and change in living creatures over time, and the impact of human activities on the web of life. Each of the mini-activities per page can be used at the beginning of class to help focus students on science-related skills. Each page can be copied and the quick starts cut apart for single use or grouping as the teacher sees fit. The pages can also be used "as is" to focus on a single subject. Quick Starts can be used any time there is a break in the class schedule to spark interest and discussion, as well as review topics that have already been taught. Quick Starts can also be kept in a learning center as enrichment activities for students who have free time.

The skills covered in each quick start activity are labeled with the following code:

O = Observing
A = Asking About
U = Understanding
F = Figuring Out
D = Doing Stuff
FO = Finding Out
M = Math Review

Review each activity before using to see if you might need any special materials or resources. This applies especially to the "Doing Stuff" activities, which are often like mini-experiments. The "Finding Out" activities might best be done in a media center where students have access to both traditional references and computers for online research. A few teacher resources are listed on page 62.

Students may need extra paper for some activities. A brief review of the metric system appears in the Math & Metrics section. It would be useful to have a variety of objects in the classroom that students could use as tools and subjects for observation. These might include magnifying lenses, prisms, metric rulers, balances for weighing objects, skulls, bones, fossils, plants, insects, dinosaur models—virtually anything to spark wonder, admiration, and interest in young (and even veteran) scientific explorers.

Diversity of Life

Diversity of Life 1 | O

List five non-human living things you have interacted with in the last 24 hours. This could include creatures like insects, mammals, birds, fish, reptiles, and microbes, as well as plants and fungi. On your own paper, explain how each organism affected your life.

_____

_____

_____

_____

_____

Diversity of Life 2 | O

Next to the living things listed below, write <u>BB</u> if they have a backbone, <u>FS</u> if they make food from sunlight, <u>ES</u> if they have an external skeleton, and <u>D</u> if they help decompose dead organisms.

_____ A. pine tree

_____ B. spider

_____ C. bat

_____ D. mushroom

_____ E. crab

_____ F. dog

Diversity of Life 3 | O

Biologists like to say "form follows function" because you can tell something about how a creature lives by their body form. Based on their structure, which of these animals:

A. lived in the water? _____

B. were predators? _____

C. ate plants? _____

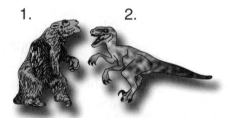

1.   2.

3.   4.   5.   6.

Diversity of Life

Diversity of Life 4   [O]

Next to each of the following arthropods, write $\underline{I}$ if it is an insect, $\underline{S}$ if it is a spider, and $\underline{N}$ if it is neither (and identify the proper class of arthropod, if you know it).

____ A. Ladybug beetle

____ B. Tarantula

____ C. Hermit crab

____ D. Jumping spider

____ E. Grasshopper

____ F. Millipede

____ G. Orb weaver

____ H. Bumblebee

Diversity of Life 5   [O]

On your own paper, draw a picture of the plant provided by your teacher and answer the following questions. Does this plant have flowers? Does it produce seeds or spores? How can you tell the difference between a seed and a spore? If your plant has flowers, draw a sketch showing the pistil, stamens, petals, and sepals.

Diversity of Life 6   [A]

Write the letter of the correct answer for the following questions about the classification of living things.

____ 1. What kingdom of creatures has no chlorophyll, reproduces with spores, and consists of mostly decomposers?

____ 2. What phylum of creatures has jointed legs, segmented bodies, and external skeletons?

A. Arthropoda
B. Protista
C. Fungi

Diversity of Life 7   [A]

On your own paper, write questions that have the following answers.

A. A biome

B. An estuary

C. A deciduous forest

D. Grasslands

Diversity of Life

Diversity of Life 8 A

Write the letter of the living thing from the list provided that best answers each riddle.

1. What takes any shape it wants, is only one cell big, and likes to ooze? ____

2. What lives on rocks and belongs to two kingdoms? ____

3. What is smaller than a blood cell, bigger than a virus,

   and sometimes has a "tail" called a flagellum? ____

A. mushroom   B. lichen   C. spore

D. amoeba   E. bacterium

Diversity of Life 9 A

Pair up with a classmate. Each of you write the name of an animal on a piece of paper and place it in an envelope. Take turns asking questions that can be answered by a "yes" or a "no." The first one to correctly guess the other's animal wins. How is asking "yes" or "no" questions similar to designing a scientific experiment?

Diversity of Life 10 A

A paleontologist discovers a new dinosaur in your backyard. What questions might you ask:

A. to find out what the dinosaur ate?

B. to find out in what kind of habitat it lived?

C. to find out to which modern animals it is most closely related?

Write your questions on another sheet of paper.

Diversity of Life

Diversity of Life 11   U

Diatoms are single-celled plants that make two-part glass shells for themselves. They float near the surface of both salt and fresh water and serve as food for many small animals.

A. Many small _____ eat diatoms for food.

B. Diatoms are plants made up of only one _____.

C. Diatoms live in _____ and _____ water.

Diversity of Life 12   U

Native Americans cultivated certain mountain grasses like teosinte and bred varieties together that had the biggest seeds. Over thousands of years, their efforts resulted in the creation of maize, better known as corn.

A. A primitive wild plant called _____ is the most likely ancestor of modern corn.

B. T or F: Maize is a kind of grass. _____

Diversity of Life 13   U

Dragonflies are insects with two pairs of transparent wings that always extend from their bodies like the stiff wings of an airplane. Their large eyes, flying skills, and spiny legs allow them to capture and kill mosquitoes and other insects for food.

A. Dragonflies make good hunters because of their _____, _____, and spiny legs.

B. T or F: Dragonflies fold their wings when at rest. _____

Diversity of Life 14   U

The oceans of the world cover an area more than twice as large as the area of all the continents combined. Scientists are performing a Census of Marine Life because they believe the oceans contain millions of unknown and undescribed species.

A. The land areas of the Earth have less than _____ the area covered by Earth's oceans.

B. T or F: Many undiscovered animals live in the oceans. _____

Diversity of Life

Diversity of Life 15   U

Tropical rain forests may contain half the land organisms on Earth, although they only cover 6% of the land area. Tropical soils are poor, however, because dead organisms decompose quickly. Most of the nutrients in a tropical forest are trapped in living trees.

A. Although rain forest soils are

_____, rain forests contain

_____ the Earth's

land organisms.

B. Most of the nutrients in

tropical forests are found

in _____.

Diversity of Life 16   F

A. To what order does a cockroach belong? _____

B. A rose by any name would be in what plant phylum?

_____

C. That chimp is no monkey! He belongs in the genus _____.

D. As a human, what's your complete classification "address" in the world of life? (kingdom, phylum, class, order, family, genus, and species)

_____

_____

_____

Diversity of Life 17   F

Write the kingdom in which the following creatures belong.

A. Green algae

_____

B. Paramecium

_____

C. Turtle

_____

D. Bread mold

_____

E. Intestinal bacterium

_____

Diversity of Life 18   F

A. What arthropod has eight eyes, book lungs, fangs, and loves to spin silk? _____

B. Which vertebrates have hollow bones, walk on two legs, and can claim *T. rex* as a distant relative?

_____

C. What do you call a hard-working female with six legs and a pollen basket who can see invisible UV light? _____

D. On your own paper, make up a riddle for your favorite mollusk.

Diversity of Life

Diversity of Life 19 $\boxed{\text{F}}$

A giant flower living in African tropical forests smells exactly like rotting flesh. What advantage might this have for the plant? How would you go about testing your hypothesis?

_____

_____

_____

_____

_____

_____

_____

Diversity of Life 20 $\boxed{\text{F}}$

I love growing on (and sometimes even inside) rocks. I come in a variety of colors from mineral green to bright orange and yellow. I have to confess, I'm not just one creature, but two, living all tangled up together.

What am I?

_____

Diversity of Life 21: Day 1 $\boxed{\text{D}}$

Create a "naturalist's notebook" for drawing pictures and making observations of plants and animals. You will need: unlined paper, a pencil, a ruler (metric, if possible), an eraser, a magnifying lens, and one natural object like a shell or twig. Draw a picture of your object. Measure its length and width. Describe how it feels and smells. Describe colors or other features your sketch doesn't show clearly. Record location, date, and time for each observation in your notebook throughout the week.

Diversity of Life 22: Day 2 $\boxed{\text{D}}$

Look carefully at an insect (or a picture of one) for one minute. Now put the insect or picture away and draw it in your notebook from memory. When you are done, look at your subject again. What did you get right? What did you miss? Can your neighbor identify the insect correctly from your drawing? Draw the insect again, referring to the picture or insect often. Why is careful observation important to really SEE something?

Diversity of Life

Diversity of Life 23: Day 3

In the schoolyard or a natural area, find an interesting plant. Sit quietly and observe it for a few minutes, then draw a careful picture in your notebook, making note of color, size, smell, and other details. Note the color and number of petals and stamens if a flower is present. What shape are the leaves? Do they have rough or smooth edges? What do the leaf veins look like? Describe and sketch how the leaves attach to the plant stem.

Diversity of Life 24: Day 4

Return to the plant you drew yesterday, or find a new one. Again, sit quietly for a while, and then record all the insects and other arthropods you see. Pay attention to things like number of body parts and legs, kind of mouthparts, wings (if present), size, color, and types of appendages on the head and tail. What exactly are the creatures doing on or near the plant?

Diversity of Life 25: Day 5

Using keys, attempt to identify all the plants and animals recorded in your notebook. Did you record the kind of information your keys refer to? If not, revisit your plant and collect any additional information you need. Were you surprised by the diversity of living things near your school? See if you can devise your own key for identifying just the creatures you found, perhaps based on things like color, number of legs, and number of body segments.

Diversity of Life 26   FO

Look up the term *diversity* in a dictionary and write its definition here.

_____

_____

_____

In the early 1990s, scientist Edward O. Wilson coined the term *biodiversity* to describe the variety of life on Earth and said, "Biological diversity is the key to the maintenance of the world as we know it." Why do you think biodiversity is important to a healthy world? Answer on your own paper.

Diversity of Life

Diversity of Life 27 FO

Spiders come in many shapes and sizes, including primitive megalomorph spiders like tarantulas, orb-weaving spiders, wolf spiders, jumping spiders, and crab spiders. Find at least one picture of each of these kinds of spider and record the publication or website where someone else can find the picture.

Tarantula: _____

Jumping spider: _____

Orb weaver: _____

Crab spider: _____

Wolf spider: _____

Diversity of Life 28 FO

A scientist once said, "We live in the Age of Beetles." Find some references on beetles in the library and look up how the number of beetle species compares with the number of species of other organisms. Explain the scientist's comment.

_____

_____

_____

_____

Diversity of Life 29 FO

Find two examples of each kind of fungus listed below.

Ascomycetes: _____

Basidiomycetes: _____

Zygomycetes: _____

What distinguishes these three kinds of fungi?

_____

_____

Energy Flow in Living Communities

Energy Flow in Living Communities 1   O

If you arrange organisms in an **energy pyramid**, **producers**, like plants that create their own food, form the base, **first-order consumers** eat producers, and **second-order consumers** (**predators**) eat those consumers. Put the letters of the following creatures in their proper spots in the energy pyramid.

A. hawk   B. prairie dog

C. grasshopper   D. grass

E. sagebrush   F. coyote

G. buffalo

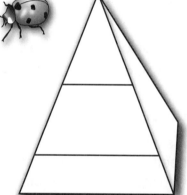

Energy Flow in Living Communities 2   O

On your own paper, make a list of all the forms of energy you have used in the last 24 hours. Which forms ultimately depend on the energy of sunlight? Did you use any nuclear or geothermal energy sources? Which sources of energy can be replenished in your lifetime?

Energy Flow in Living Communities 3   O

A **food chain** consists of the sequence of producers (usually green plants) and the animals that eat them and each other. On your own paper, draw a food chain that includes you and the various plants and animals you eat when you order your favorite pizza. (Don't forget the components of the sauce and the crust).

Energy Flow in Living Communities

Energy Flow in Living Communities 4   O

Food webs consist of all the inter-linked food chains in an ecosystem. Create a food web built from at least six plants and six animals that live near you. In what way are you "outside" the local food web? Draw the food web on your own paper.

Energy Flow in Living Communities 5   O

Keystone species are organisms so important to an ecosystem that the system would fall apart without them. On your own paper, make a list of several plants and animals that might be considered keystone species where you live. Explain your choices. In what ways are common soil microbes (**decomposers**) keystone species?

Energy Flow in Living Communities 6   A

A space probe discovers a new planet. The probe can't land, but it can analyze the composition

of the atmosphere. What questions would you ask to decide if the planet possessed a living biosphere? Write the questions on your own paper.

Energy Flow in Living Communities 7   A

On your own paper, write questions that have the following answers.

A. Transpiration

B. Precipitation

C. Fossil fuels

D. Respiration

Energy Flow in Living Communities

Energy Flow in Living Communities 8

Match the questions with the letter of the best answer.

_____ 1. What is the energy-producing organelle in a cell?

_____ 2. What organelle helps break down a dead cell?

_____ 3. What organelle helps assemble proteins?

A. Nucleus   B. Ribosome
C. Lysosome   D. Mitochondrion

Energy Flow in Living Communities 9

A. What is the chemical formula for green plant photosynthesis?

_____

_____

B. What is the chemical formula for respiration in plants and animals?

_____

_____

C. How are these formulas similar?

_____

_____

_____

_____

Energy Flow in Living Communities 10

Answer on your own paper.

A. What phase of cell division has all the chromosomes lined up in the middle of the cell?

B. During what phase of cell division do chromosomes pull apart?

C. During what phase of cell division does the nuclear membrane disappear?

D. How does meiosis differ from mitosis?

Energy Flow in Living Communities 11

Most organisms on Earth get energy from the sun—either directly like plants or indirectly like the animals that eat plants and the microorganisms that decompose them. Some primitive microorganisms like sulfur bacteria can use sulfur and carbon dioxide to make energy.

A. T or F: All organisms derive energy from the sun. _____

B. T or F: Sulfur can be a source of energy for some organisms. _____

Energy Flow in Living Communities

Energy Flow in Living Communities 12

In the 18th century, Joseph Priestley discovered that a burning candle would go out when sealed in a glass container unless he put a sprig of mint in with it. Researchers discovered that green plants produced oxygen that the candle needed in order to burn.

A. Plants produce _____, an element needed for something to burn.

B. Would a candle burn in a sealed jar with a mint plant in a dark room? _____ Explain:

_____

_____

Energy Flow in Living Communities 13

A living cell uses a molecule called adenosine triphosphate (ATP) to store energy in chemical bonds. When those bonds break, energy is released to do the work of the cell.

A. Cellular energy is stored in chemical bonds in a molecule called

_____

_____.

B. T or F: When ATP bonds break, the cells receive energy to perform useful work. _____

Energy Flow in Living Communities 14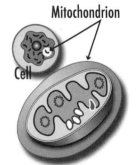

Mitochondria are cell organelles that produce most of a plant or animal's energy during the process of respiration. Mitochondria are believed to have once been free-living bacteria that formed a symbiotic relationship with the ancestors of modern plants and animals.

A. Energy is produced in cell organelles called

_____.

B. Mitochondria may once have been free-living

_____.

C. Respiration is a cellular process resulting in the production of

_____.

Energy Flow in Living Communities

Energy Flow in Living Communities 15   U

A gas, like oxygen, which readily combines with other elements, can only exist in a planet's atmosphere if it is constantly replaced through a process like photosynthesis, carried on by living plants.

A. Planets with life may have atmospheres with large amounts of _____.

B. On a planet where all oxygen is trapped in rocks, scientists would (expect / not expect) to find life.

Energy Flow in Living Communities 16   F

In prehistoric times in the Great Interior Seaway of North America, a huge aquatic lizard called a mosasaur ate an ammonite that had just eaten a fish that had eaten a crab that had eaten an amoeba that had eaten a single-celled plant. On your own paper, draw a picture of a food chain showing this event and indicate where energy is lost.

A. Who is the top predator in this chain? _____

B. Which creature would come from the largest population of individuals? _____

Energy Flow in Living Communities 17   F

I am a high-powered molecule with phosphate bonds loaded with energy. I hang out with my buddies near mitochondria.

What's my name?

_____

_____

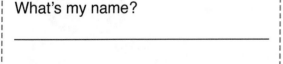

Energy Flow in Living Communities 18   F

Match the cell organelle with the job it performs.

____ 1. Controls what enters and leaves the nucleus

____ 2. Site for protein manufacture

____ 3. Breaks down cell structure

____ 4. Membrane network within a cell

A. Endoplasmic reticulum
B. Lysosome
C. Centriole
D. Ribosome
E. Nuclear Membrane

Energy Flow in Living Communities

Energy Flow in Living Communities 19   F

On Mars, scientists have recently discovered small amounts of methane. They believe this might indicate Mars has life. Why might they make this hypothesis? What else could explain the methane? Write your answers on your own paper.

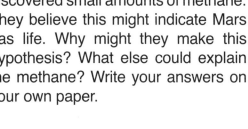

Energy Flow in Living Communities 20   F

Which of the following energy sources is least likely to be available in 1,000 years? _____

A. Geothermal   B. Nuclear
C. Oil   D. Solar

Explain your answer.

_____

_____

_____

_____

_____

Energy Flow in Living Communities 21: Day 1   D

Divide into four groups. Those in group 1 make a list of all the insects you can think of. Those in group 2 make a list of things insects eat. Those in group 3 make a list of all the organisms that eat insects. Group 4 people make a list of eaters of insect eaters. Save your lists for tomorrow.

Energy Flow in Living Communities 22: Day 2   D

Find pictures of or draw as many of the animals and/or plants on your list from Day 1's Quick Start as you can. Your teacher will provide old nature magazines to cut up or pictures of insects that can be drawn on 3″ x 5″ cards.

Energy Flow in Living Communities

Energy Flow in Living Communities 23: Day 3

Your teacher will be the sun—the ultimate source of energy for most living communities (ecosystems). Every student represents one of the animals or plants on their group's list. The teacher will hold the free end of a ball of string representing the sun's energy. She will throw the ball to someone in Group 2 representing a plant. That person holds the string and throws the ball to the plant's insect consumer. Continue to the end of the food chain. Repeat for several food chains. A network of food chains makes a food web and shows how complex ecosystems can be.

Energy Flow in Living Communities 24: Day 4

You will need 4 pizza boxes: large, medium, small, and single-serving size. Group 2 should paste all their pictures on the lid of the large pizza box. Group 1 pastes their pictures on the medium pizza box. Group 3 gets the small pizza box, and Group 4 uses the single-serving box. Stack the boxes on top of each other so that they form a pyramid. Draw a picture of the pyramid and list all the animals and plants pasted on each box.

Energy Flow in Living Communities 25: Day 5

Think about your pizza-box food pyramid, and answer the following questions on your own paper.

A. What kinds of organisms comprise the base of the pyramid? Why are there more of them?
B. Which levels of the pyramid have consumers?
C. Which level in the pyramid has most of the sun's energy?
D. Decomposers are not represented in this model. What role do they play in an ecosystem?

Energy Flow in Living Communities 26

Indicate whether the following freshwater insects are herbivores (H), carnivores (C), or omnivores (O):

Mayfly larva _____
Stonefly nymph _____
Caddisfly nymph _____
Dragonfly adult _____
Dragonfly nymph _____

What did you use to research your answers?

_____

_____

Energy Flow in Living Communities

Energy Flow in Living Communities 27

The inert gas nitrogen makes up 78% of the earth's atmosphere. What role does it play in keeping Earth's biosphere healthy? (Answer on your own paper.)

The answer to this question and others can be found at <http://www.nas.nasa.gov/Services/Education/SpaceSettlement/designer/needs.html>, a website that discusses the needs of a permanent colony in space. What other needs does this site mention for a space settlement?

Energy Flow in Living Communities 28

Male assassin bugs guard their eggs and protect them from parasitic wasps, but it's a full-time job until the eggs hatch, so males will eat some of their own eggs. Explain how this practice helps insure the survival of assassin bugs.

_____

_____

_____

Where could you find more information about assassin bugs?

_____

Energy Flow in Living Communities 29

On your own paper, define the following terms.

A. Enzyme

B. Catalyst

C. Carbohydrate

D. Ribosomal RNA

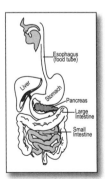

Energy Flow in Living Communities 30

American pronghorns can run 60 miles per hour and leap 20 feet. No modern predators can catch them. Pronghorns may have evolved their running in response to predators that lived during the ice age. Research some of the animals that lived during this time that might have made pronghorns "run for their lives." Look up the following creatures: short-faced bear, saber-toothed cat, cheetah, dire wolf, giant lion (*Panthera*), and jaguar.

Which ones may have been fast runners? How do paleontologists know? Answer on your own paper.

Organization of the Human Body

Organization of the Human Body 1   [O]

You will need a watch or a clock with a minute hand. Place an index finger either below and just behind your ear or on your writst until you feel the throb of your pulse. Count the number of pulses per minute three different times.

A. sitting _____   B. standing _____

C. after running in place for 30 seconds _____

D. How did your pulse change? _____

E. What causes your pulse? _____

_____

Organization of the Human Body 2   [O]

Cut a strip of paper about 2.5″ wide and 6″ long. Hold the paper with your left hand at the top corner of a narrow end. Place your right thumb and forefinger on either side of the bottom of the paper without holding it. Release the paper with your left hand. You should have no trouble catching it with your right hand. Hold the paper a second time with someone else's hand ready to catch it. Release the paper without telling them when you are going to do it, and it will probably slip through their fingers. Why?

_____

_____

Organization of the Human Body 3   [O]

Using a mirror, open your mouth and look at your teeth. The four front ones on top and bottom are called **incisors**. The pointed teeth just behind them are called "eye teeth," or **canines**. The rest of the teeth are **molars**. On your own paper, sketch the shape of these different teeth. Based on their size and shape, what different "jobs" do they have when you eat?

_____

_____

_____

Organization of the Human Body

Organization of the Human Body 4 ☐O

Hold your hands about three inches away from your eyes, and touch your two index fingers together. Now focus on a distant wall while you move your fingers about a half-inch apart. Glance back at your fingers and you will see a "floating finger" between your index fingers! See if you can explain this optical illusion.

_____

_____

_____

_____

Organization of the Human Body 5 ☐O

You will need water, two cotton balls, and rubbing alcohol.
Moisten one cotton ball with water and rub on your left forearm. Moisten the other cotton ball with rubbing alcohol and rub on your right forearm. Which forearm feels cooler? Why? Why might a doctor have prescribed an "alcohol bath" for someone in the past?

_____

_____

_____

Organization of the Human Body 6 ☐A

What system in the human body…

A. Controls the response to invading microorganisms?

_____

B. Provides for gas exchange between the air and the body?

_____

C. Breaks down food and absorbs nutrients?

_____

D. Provides support and stores minerals?

_____

Organization of the Human Body 7 ☐A

On your own paper, write questions that have the following answers.

A. A, B, O, and AB

B. White blood cells

C. Left and right ventricles

Organization of the Human Body

Organization of the Human Body 8

What digestive system organ best solves each riddle below? Place the letter of the correct organ on the blank next to each riddle.

1. What has peristaltic waves but no sunny beaches? _____

2. What is small and twisty and a whiz at digestion? _____

3. What is home to friendly microbes and loves to soak up water? _____

   A. Pancreas   B. Mouth   C. Large intestine

   D. Small intestine   E. Esophagus

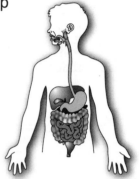

Organization of the Human Body 9

On your own paper, write riddles about the following endocrine glands that include enough information about their functions that someone could identify the proper gland correctly.

A. Thyroid gland
B. Hypothalamus
C. Adrenal gland
D. Thymus gland

Organization of the Human Body 10

Find a partner. Each of you write the name of one of the 206 human bones on a piece of paper and put the paper in an envelope. Each of you may ask ten questions that can be answered with a "yes" or a "no." What are the mystery bones?

Organization of the Human Body

Organization of the Human Body 11 U

Of the 100 trillion cells inside us, only one in ten is human. The rest belong to bacteria, fungi, viruses, and micro-scopic insects—many of them either "hitchhikers" or symbionts performing valuable services to keep us healthy.

A. T or F: All microorganisms cause disease. _____

B. Organisms that live on or in the hu-man body include _____, _____, _____, and _____.

Organization of the Human Body 12 U

The form of a human cell reflects the function it performs. Muscle cells are long with fibers that contract. Nerve cells have many branches (dendrites) and insulated axons for transmitting nerve impulses. White blood cells have bumpy extensions that surround foreign invaders.

A. T or F: A skin cell is flat and plate-like to provide protection. _____

B. Muscle cells have fibers that can _____ like an entire muscle.

Organization of the Human Body 13 U

A blocked blood vessel that serves the brain may cause a stroke. A blocked blood vessel in the heart starves the heart muscle and causes a heart attack. A weak-walled blood vessel may expand into a bulge called an aneurysm that may burst.

A. Blood vessels can become blocked in the brain, causing a _____.

B. Blood vessels may burst if an _____ is present.

Organization of the Human Body 14 U

Human blood consists of solids such as white cells, red cells, and cell frag-ments called platelets floating in a fluid called plasma. Plasma is 90% water and 10% sugars, fats, salts, gases, and proteins that determine human blood groups.

A. Human blood contains solids like _____, _____, and _____.

B. Sugars, fats, and other chemicals make up _____% of blood plasma.

Organization of the Human Body

Organization of the Human Body 15

The central nervous system (CNS) consists of the brain and spinal cord. The brain is divided into the medulla that takes care of "autopilot" functions, the cerebellum that handles coordination and balance, and the cerebrum that understands passages of text like this one.

A. Use your _____ to read this activity,

your _____ to walk to the gym, and your

_____ to keep your heart beating.

B. CNS stands for _____ _____ _____ .

Organization of the Human Body 16

Draw a line connecting the part of the nervous system with the function it performs.

A. Interneurons   carry out CNS commands.

B. Motor neurons   transmit signals from receptors.

C. Sensory neurons   connect sensory & motor neurons.

D. Effectors   is the main nerve trunk line.

E. Spinal cord   innervate muscles.

Organization of the Human Body 17

Next to the following human diseases write <u>I</u> if it is infectious and <u>NI</u> if it is not infectious. Be prepared to explain your answers.

A. Diabetes mellitus ____

B. Scurvy ____

C. Yellow fever ____

D. HIV ____

E. Cancer ____

Organization of the Human Body

Organization of the Human Body 18

I live in a bean-shaped organ deep within the body. I filter wastes from the blood while cleverly reabsorbing certain nutrients, salts, and water. I hang around with a bunch of my tubular buddies in a structure called a capsule.

What am I? _____

Organization of the Human Body 19

On your own paper, make up a riddle about each of the following structures in the human respiratory system. Try them out on a classmate and see if he or she can figure them out.

A. Alveolus
B. Epiglottis
C. Nasal cavity
D. Larynx

Organization of the Human Body 20

Microscopic invaders have entered your body. They cruise around in the blood until they find T-cells and then they destroy them. What will happen in your body if you don't find a way to replace T-cells?

_____

_____

_____

_____

_____

_____

Organization of the Human Body 21

With a soft-leaded pencil, make a solid circle of pencil lead (graphite) about 1″ in diameter. Rub your left index finger on the graphite. Tear off about an inch of clear tape with your right hand and place it, sticky side down, on your left index finger. Remove the tape and stick it on a piece of white paper. Observe the whorled patterns of your fingerprint with a hand lens, if available. Fingerprints are unique for each person. How does yours compare with your neighbors'?

Organization of the Human Body

Organization of the Human Body 22

D

On a piece of paper, draw two $\frac{1}{4}$-inch black dots 4 inches apart. Hold the paper at arm's length from your eyes. Close your right eye and look at the right dot on the paper with your left eye. Move the paper slowly toward your face. Stop moving the paper when the left dot disappears. Why do you think you have this "blind spot" in your vision? Refer to the diagram of a human eye at right for ideas.

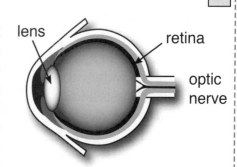

lens   retina   optic nerve

_____

_____

_____

_____

_____

Organization of the Human Body 23

D

Some human traits are determined by a single pair of genes, such as free-hanging earlobes versus attached earlobes.

A. What percentage of people in your class has free-hanging earlobes?

_____

B. Which kind of earlobe is most likely determined by a **dominant** gene? _____

Organization of the Human Body 24

D

Fool your brain! Find a partner and place the palms of your left hands together. With the thumb and forefinger of your free hand rub the outsides of your joined left index fingers at the same time. What does the sensation feel like? Why is your brain getting fooled into thinking half of your finger is asleep?

Organization of the Human Body

Organization of the Human Body 25 [D]

Read the words in List A three times. Cover the list and try to rewrite it in the correct order on a blank piece of paper. Repeat the process for Lists B and C.

List A: ter, coz, bim, tur, bof, sop

List B: rigid, tunnel, cow, hammer, toad, funnel

List C: rake, the, lawn, please, uncle, sam

On which list did you get the most words in the correct order? Why?

_____

_____

How might you make it easier on yourself to memorize a list of vocabulary words? _____

_____

_____

Organization of the Human Body 26 [FO]

If someone's body cannot produce the blood protein **fibrin,** what problems would you expect them to have?

_____

_____

_____

What resources did you use to answer this question?

_____

_____

_____

Organization of the Human Body 27 [FO]

What are the roles of the following hormones in human sexual development? Answer on your own paper.

A. Estrogen

B. Progesterone

C. Testosterone

Organization of the Human Body

Organization of the Human Body 28

FO

Answer the following on your own paper.

A. Explain the difference between active immunity and passive immunity.

B. What are the roles of phagocytes, T-cells, and B-cells in active immunity?

Organization of the Human Body 29

FO

In 2007, a vaccine was discovered that is 96% effective against hepatitis E.

A. What human organ does hepatitis E attack? _____

B. What kind of organism causes hepatitis E? _____

C. Hepatitis E has been estimated to infect up to one-third of the world's population. What impacts does a discovery like this one have on people's lives? _____

_____

_____

Organization of the Human Body 30

FO

Mad cow disease and scrapie are infectious diseases of livestock that affect the brain. People develop something similar called Creutzfeldt-Jakob disease (CJD). Biological agents called **prions** cause all these diseases. Use an Internet search engine to look up prions.

How do prions differ from bacteria and viruses? How do they cause damage in the brain? _____

_____

_____

Life Cycles of Organisms

Life Cycles of Organisms 1   O

Look carefully at the close-up pictures of an adult and immature butterfly. Mark each statement below as true (T) or false (F).

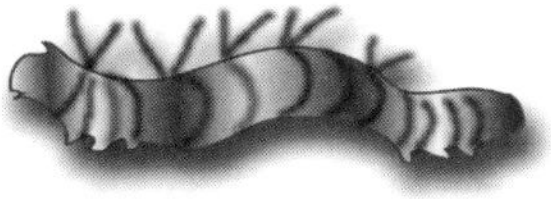

____ A. Butterflies and their caterpillars eat different things.

____ B. Butterflies show incomplete metamorphosis.

Life Cycles of Organisms 2   O

Research the life cycle of a chinch bug and a ladybug. Which insect shows a kind of development called complete metamorphosis?

_____

Explain what that term means.

_____

_____

_____

_____

_____

Life Cycles of Organisms 3   O

Label the parts of a corn seedling shown below.

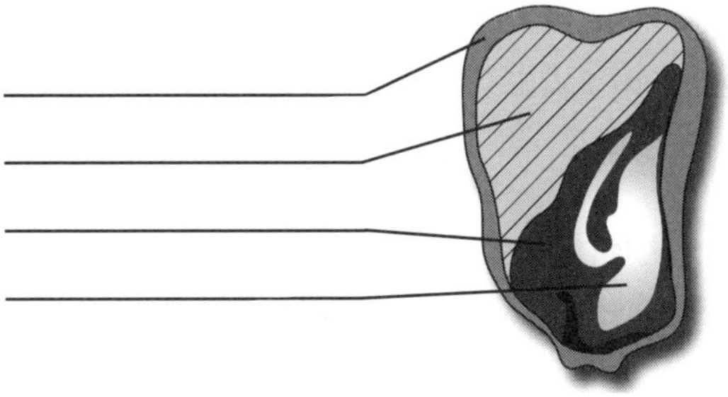

What does the endosperm do?

_____

_____

_____

_____

Life Cycles of Organisms 4   O

Look at the pictures of an adult tiger salamander (top) and a young or larval tiger salamander, called an **axolotl** (bottom).

Where do you think the axolotl lives?

_____

_____

_____

_____

Life Cycles of Organisms

Life Cycles of Organisms 5

O

Look at the illustrations of four different plants showing their roots, stems, leaves, and flowers.

1.   2.

3.   4.

A. Which plants have roots we can eat? _____

B. Which plant has the biggest flower? _____

C. Which plants have seeds we can eat? _____

D. Which plant has finely divided leaves? _____

Life Cycles of Organisms 6

A

If you were a rose…

A. would you be a monocot or a dicot? _____

B. would you be an angiosperm or a gymnosperm? _____

C. what would your male gametes be called? _____

D. where would I find your sepals? _____

Life Cycles of Organisms 7

A

Place the letter of the correct answer on the blank next to each question.

_____ 1. What is a hollow ball of cells called in early animal development?

_____ 2. What tissue eventually forms muscles?

_____ 3. What tissue forms nerve cells?

_____ 4. What tissue forms the digestive system?

A. Gastrula   B. Endoderm   C. Ectoderm

D. Mesoderm   E. Blastula

Life Cycles of Organisms

Life Cycles of Organisms 8

On your own paper, write questions that have the following answers.

A. Alternation of generations

B. Gametophyte

C. Sporophyte

D. Annulus

Life Cycles of Organisms 9

What advantages might there be for insects with complete metamorphosis over those with incomplete metamorphosis when food supplies are limited? How could you test your hypothesis? Answer on your own paper.

Life Cycles of Organisms 10

See if you can answer the ancient Greek "Riddle of the Sphinx":

"What goes on four legs in the morning, two legs at noon, and three legs in the evening?"

_____

(Hint: The riddle is a metaphor and has something to do with human development.)

Make up a similar riddle for a butterfly on your own paper.

Life Cycles of Organisms 11 U

Roly poly or pill bugs are a kind of crustacean that lives on land. These creatures roll up into a ball for protection and to conserve water loss. Females carry young in brood pouches that grow from their legs.

A. A pill bug rolls up for two reasons. What are they?

_____

_____

B. Female pill bugs carry their young in _____.

Life Cycles of Organisms

Life Cycles of Organisms 12 U

Green lacewing adults lay their eggs on top of long stalks on roses and other plants infested with aphids. Aphids eat plant juices. Lacewing larvae, called aphid lions, have huge jaws that they use to capture and eat aphids.

A. Aphid lions are the larvae of insects called _____.

B. It would probably be safe to say that lacewings (help / hurt) the plants on which they lay their eggs.

Life Cycles of Organisms 13 U

Slime molds are one-celled amoeba-like creatures that, when conditions are right, send out a chemical signal that attracts others of their kind. The cells gather and fuse to form a body that produces spores. The spores germinate on forest soil into new, crawling slime mold cells.

A. Slime molds are single-celled until they send out a _____ that attracts other slime molds.

B. Slime molds reproduce by forming a body that makes _____.

Life Cycles of Organisms 14 U

The Colorado potato beetle used to live on a plant called buffalo bur, a relative of the potato that grew in the mud near buffalo wallows. When farmers grew large tracts of potatoes, the beetle became a pest by eating and living on potato plants.

A. T or F: Potato beetles can feed on more than one plant. _____

B. Buffalo bur is a relative of _____.

Life Cycles of Organisms 15 U

Female mosquitoes bite humans and other animals for the blood meals they need to lay their eggs and reproduce. In the process, they transmit the deadly diseases malaria and yellow fever.

A. Mosquitoes transmit diseases like _____ and _____.

B. Blood serves as _____ for female mosquitoes and gives them the energy to _____.

Life Cycles of Organisms

Life Cycles of Organisms 16

Fleas are wingless insects that suck blood for food and have great leaping abilities. This information may help you solve the following riddles.

A. Where do fleas keep their money?

_____

B. What happens when you play checkers with a flea?

_____

C. What happens when a flea loses its temper?

_____

Life Cycles of Organisms 17

Below are the immature stages of a common amphibian.

A.   B.

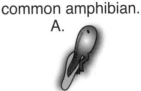

C.   D.

A. Write the letters of the stages in the order they would occur:

_____ _____ _____ _____

B. What is the adult animal called?

_____

Life Cycles of Organisms 18

A mosquito finds a creature to bite by sensing the carbon dioxide it gives off. Recently, scientists have found two mosquito genes that appear to be responsible for this ability. On your own paper, describe how scientists might go about devising new mosquito repellents using this knowledge.

Life Cycles of Organisms 19

On a rose flower…
A. Where would you find male reproductive cells?

_____

B. Where would you find female reproductive cells?

_____

C. What does a pollen tube do?

_____

_____

D. Where would you find sepals?

_____

_____

Life Cycles of Organisms

Life Cycles of Organisms 20

F

Match the monarch butterfly life stage with the proper description.

____ 1. Responsible for laying eggs

____ 2. Must eat lots of milkweed

____ 3. Rests and regroups for winter

____ 4. White body with black head

____ 5. Found beneath milkweed leaves

a. Immature larva

b. Adult butterfly

c. Eggs

d. Mature caterpillar

e. Pupa

Life Cycles of Organisms 21: Session 1

D

Your teacher will supply a colony of mealworms, the larvae of grain beetles (*Tenebrio molitor*) used for pet food. Keep the larvae in small plastic tubs half full of oat bran. Now and then add a small piece of potato for moisture. Over several weeks, you will see them complete their life cycle.

Draw careful pictures of a larva, pupa, and adult, measuring their lengths in millimeters. Answer all questions for these activities on your own paper.

Life Cycles of Organisms 22: Session 2

D

How fast do larvae grow? Isolate a young larva (almost white in color) in a small dish of bran. Measure the larva's length in millimeters each day until it turns into a pupa and record your results in a chart.

Divide the increase in length from the first day to the last day of measurements by the number of days. What is your larva's growth rate in millimeters/day?

How does it compare with that of other students? What factors might affect growth rate?

Life Cycles of Organisms

Life Cycles of Organisms 23: Session 3

Do adult and larval *Tenebrio* prefer being in the light or the dark? Write down your prediction (hypothesis).

Materials: Petri dishes, black paper, scissors, tape, paper, and pencil.

Work in small groups. Cover half of the top lid of two Petri dishes with black paper. Place a Tenebrio adult in the center of the bottom of one Petri dish and a larva in the same position in the second dish. Cover each bottom with a half-darkened top lid. After a half hour, record whether the adult and larva are under the dark or light half of the lid. Compile the class results in a bar graph. Was your hypothesis supported?

Life Cycles of Organisms 24: Session 4

Are *Tenebrio* adults attracted to cold or warmth? What is your hypothesis?

Get a long baking tray. Put a heating pad under one end and a tray of ice cubes under the other. Wait one-half hour. Put several beetles in the middle of the tray. After half an hour, record the location of the beetles.

 What are your conclusions? What would make you more confident that your conclusions are correct?

Life Cycles of Organisms 25: Session 5

Do *Tenebrio* larvae or adults prefer dampness to dryness? How does temperature affect their growth rate? How does the kind of food or the amount of food affect growth rate? Do adults and larvae prefer being on a dark or light substrate?

Select one of these questions or one of your own, make a hypothesis, and design an experiment to test that hypothesis.

Why would farmers like to know about *Tenebrio* behavior?

Life Cycles of Organisms

Life Cycles of Organisms 26 FO

Science fiction often gets its ideas for monsters from down-to-earth creatures.

On your own paper, compare and contrast one or both of the following:

1. Ant lions (insect order "Neuroptera," family "Myrmeleontidae") and the creature at the bottom of Sarlacc's Pit in *Star Wars: Return of the Jedi.*

2. Parasitic wasps and the creature in *Alien.*

Life Cycles of Organisms 27 FO

The larvae of dragonflies are voracious predators, with a hinged jaw that covers their face like a mask until suitable prey swims too close. Then the jaw quickly extends out to grab lunch.

Find pictures of several dragonfly larvae and design an alien "monster" with a similar life cycle. Either draw a picture or construct a model. Write a short description of the specifics of the alien's world and habitat.

Life Cycles of Organisms 28 FO

About 70 vertebrate species can sometimes reproduce without the help of a male. So far, these include certain reptiles, amphibians, fish, and birds, but no mammals. Most recently, scientists found that Komodo dragon females can produce viable eggs without males.

Research this process called **parthenogenesis** and explain on your own paper how it works.

Life Cycles of Organisms 29 FO

Some plants eat meat, usually in the form of insects. Examples include pitcher plants and venus fly traps.

Research and draw the life cycle of a carnivorous plant on your own paper.

What environmental conditions have led to the evolution of carnivorous plants?

A good website to visit is <http://www. botany.org/carnivorous_plants/index. php.>

Descent & Change Over Time

Descent & Change Over Time 1 　O

Look at the four pictures of Marvin (all drawn to the same scale) as a baby, a child, a teenager, and adult. Answer the following questions on your own paper.

Measure the total height of each figure. How many times taller is the adult Marvin than baby Marvin?

Measure the height of Marvin's baby head and divide by the baby's height. Do the same for the other figures.

Explain how body proportions change with age.

Descent & Change Over Time 2 　O

A population of moths has some light-colored forms and others that are dark. If the trunks of all trees in a forest are blackened during a fire, which color moth will survive in greater numbers? How will this change the frequency of white and dark moths in the next generation? Answer on your own paper.

Descent & Change Over Time 3 　O

Use the Internet or other resource to compare the skeleton of *Tyrannosaurus rex* with the following modern animals: a bird, an amphibian, and a cat. Which does the *T. rex* skeleton most resemble?

_____

In China, fossils of small dinosaurs have been found with the impressions of feathers. Does this fact support your choice?

_____

Descent & Change Over Time

Descent & Change Over Time 4

Modern horses are different from ancient horses. Look at the scale drawings of the leg bones of modern and ancient horses, and name at least two things that have changed.

1. _____

2. _____

Descent & Change Over Time 5

In eastern Colorado, the following fossils are commonly found near the prairie town of Pueblo: giant clams, squid-like creatures, fish, and giant sea reptiles. Mark the following statements as true (T) or false (F).

____ A. Colorado's climate has always been the same.

____ B. Colorado must have had an ocean at one time.

____ C. The prairie would be a good place to find living clams.

Descent & Change Over Time 6

Place the letter of the correct answer next to each question.

____ 1. What are the basic units of heredity called?

____ 2. On what cell structures do you find genes?

____ 3. What is an organism's overall appearance called?

A. Chromosomes   B. Genotype

C. Phenotype   D. Genes

Descent & Change Over Time 7

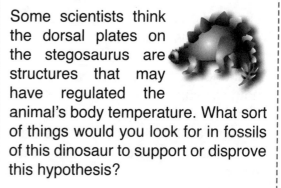

Some scientists think the dorsal plates on the stegosaurus are structures that may have regulated the animal's body temperature. What sort of things would you look for in fossils of this dinosaur to support or disprove this hypothesis?

_____

_____

_____

_____

Descent & Change Over Time

Descent & Change Over Time 8

At the right is a geological cross section of a sequence of rocks.

1. A, B, and C are fossils.

   Which one is oldest? _____

   Why? _____

   _____

   _____

2. What is D called?

   _____

3. What happened along the line XY?

   _____

   _____

   _____

A.

B.

D.

Y.

X.

C.

Descent & Change Over Time 9

While building a new house in your neighborhood, the fossilized remains of an animal are found. What questions would you ask an expert about the remains…

A. to find out the age of the fossil?
B. to find out the kind of things it ate?
C. to find out how it was related to modern animals?

Write the questions on your own paper.

Descent & Change Over Time 10

Allele "Y" is the dominant allele for yellow flower color. A plant with two "y" alleles will be white. If a plant with genotype "Yy" is crossed with a plant of genotype "yy,"…

A. What percentage of the offspring will be white? _____

B. What percentage will have the genotype "YY"? _____

Descent & Change Over Time

Descent & Change Over Time 11

Thomas Jefferson, third president of the United States, studied the fossils of giant mastodons found in Kentucky and elsewhere. Because most of the United States was unexplored in the eighteenth century, he hoped the explorers Lewis and Clark would find live examples of mastodons on their western travels.

A. In the 18th century, much of the _____

_____ was unexplored.

B. President _____

studied fossil remains of _____.

Descent & Change Over Time 12

In 1922, Roy Chapman Andrews found the first examples of dinosaur eggs in the Gobi Desert in Mongolia. He thought the eggs belonged to protoceratops, but later, similar eggs were found in a nest with their true dinosaur mother, the oviraptor.

A. Dinosaur eggs were first found in _____ in 1922.

B. T or F: The eggs discovered by Andrews belonged to the dinosaur

protoceratops. ____

Descent & Change Over Time 13

Radical changes in fossils mark major disasters in the history of life. Many years ago, an asteroid probably struck the Earth, destroying the world of the dinosaurs and allowing surviving mammals to adapt and change into new species.

A. You would expect fossils from after the asteroid strike to be

(different / the same as) fossils from before the strike.

B. Fossils show that Earth sometimes suffers major _____.

Descent & Change Over Time

Descent & Change Over Time 14

U

Whales once had legs. Fossils of whale relatives have been found in Pakistan with well-developed arms and legs. Modern whales have tiny hip and leg bones deep within their streamlined bodies.

A. _____ and _____ bones in modern whales are remnants of the functioning legs of their ancestors.

B. T or F: Modern whales can be found in Pakistan. _____

Descent & Change Over Time 15

U

When people stop taking antibiotics too soon, the tough bacteria that survive reproduce to create "super bug" populations resistant to the antibiotic used.

A. T or F: Bacterial populations change as a result of exposure to antibiotics. _____

B. Stopping antibiotic treatment too soon results in bacteria _____ to the antibiotic.

Descent & Change Over Time 16

F

A unique species of single-celled plant (a diatom) was found in Yellowstone Lake. 14,000-year-old fossils of the same diatom found in the lake's sediment look similar to diatoms from neighboring lakes. Pollen studies show the climate then was cooler and wetter. On your own paper, make a hypothesis about what may have happened to the population of diatoms in Yellowstone Lake over 14,000 years ago. What factors cause isolated populations to change over time?

Descent & Change Over Time 17

F

Some people can't digest cow's milk because their bodies don't have the enzyme necessary to break down milk sugar (lactose). People descended from traditional cattle herders are much more likely to be able to digest milk sugar. On your own paper, explain how this may have happened over time. Of what process is this an example?

Descent & Change Over Time

Descent & Change Over Time 18

While most mammoths died out nearly 10,000 years ago, fossils of a pygmy variety of mammoth were found on Russia's Wrangel Island that may have survived until 1,500 B.C. Creatures often develop into dwarf varieties when they colonize islands. What would be the advantages of being small in size on an island?

_____

_____

_____

_____

Descent & Change Over Time 19

In the Late Cretaceous Period of North America, many species of large, herbivorous dinosaurs called hadrosaurs lived in the same habitat. Each species had distinctive crests or horns on their skulls. What function might these head ornaments have had? What would you look for in the fossil record to test your ideas? Answer on your own paper.

Descent & Change Over Time 20

Match the term with the correct description.

____ 1. Tendency of gene frequencies to change randomly

____ 2. Reproduction by the most fit creatures

____ 3. Natural differences in members of a population

____ 4. Mountains, rivers, and even behavioral differences can result in this.

A. Isolation   B. Genetic drift   C. Natural selection   D. Variation

Descent & Change Over Time

Descent & Change Over Time 21

Over time, water wears away the earth's surface in some places and builds it up in others. How does this take place? Gather the following materials and perform the experiment to find out.

Materials Needed: sand and clay   large tray   watering can

Step 1:   Build up a pile of sand and clay in a tray or other large vessel.

Step 2:   Sprinkle it gently with a watering can. Note the erosion, the transportation of rock particles, and deposits made by the little streams that form.

Why might a fossil formed in one location be found in a completely different location many years later?

_____

_____

_____

Descent & Change Over Time 22

By comparing fossil skeletons and tracks, scientists know that the height of a dinosaur from foot to hip is roughly equal to four times its footprint length. The head-to-tail length is ten times footprint length. The *T. rex* named Sue at the Chicago Field Museum is 41 feet long.

A. How long a footprint would she have made? _____

B. What hip height would you expect her to have? _____

Descent & Change Over Time 23

Creatures can become preserved as fossils by being frozen, mummified, trapped in tar or amber, and mineralized (petrified) after burial. Their bodies can also be preserved as casts or molds or turned into a thin film of carbon by heat and pressure. Living things also leave trace fossils like tracks and fossil poop. Discuss the best way for someone to become a "future fossil," if they so desired.

Descent & Change Over Time

Descent & Change Over Time 24

If you bury a piece of sponge in a bowl of sand, pour salt water into the bowl, and then let the water evaporate, the sponge will be hard when you dig it up because salt crystallizes in the sponge pores. How is this similar to bones being buried and then becoming petrified fossils?

_____

_____

_____

_____

_____

Descent & Change Over Time 25

Imagine you had the same bedroom for your entire life, and it was never cleaned. What would some future archeologist find near the bottom of your room? What would she find in the middle and near the top? What might cause the "layers" to get mixed up?

On your own paper, write a fictional report of the archeologist's findings and her conclusions about the bedroom's occupant.

Descent & Change Over Time 26

In the movie *Jurassic Park*, scientists used DNA in the guts of mosquitoes trapped in amber to recreate dinosaurs.

Answer these questions on your own paper.

A. What is amber?
B. What kinds of creatures have been found trapped in amber?
C. What difficulties would scientists have in trying to recreate dinosaurs like they did in the movie?

Descent & Change Over Time 27

The Denver Museum of Nature and Science has an award-winning exhibition called "Prehistoric Journey" that shows what Colorado looked like in the distant past. Visit <http://www.dmns.org/exhibitions/current-exhibitions/prehistoric-journey/>, and click on the Prehistoric Journey Exhibit Activity Guide. Read through the information and find the name of the ostrich-like animal from the Cretaceous Period, 66 million years ago.

_____

Descent & Change Over Time

Descent & Change Over Time 28

FO

Scientists believe that mountain-dwelling relatives of rabbits called picas may become extinct within the next hundred years due to global warming.

A. What does it mean when an animal becomes extinct?

_____

_____

B. How could global warming cause the extinction of picas?

_____

_____

_____

Descent & Change Over Time 29

FO

In the nineteenth century, a feud between two paleontologists resulted in the discovery of many dinosaurs in the American West. The clashes between Edward Drinker Cope and Othniel Marsh are sometimes referred to as "the dinosaur wars." On your own paper, list two dinosaurs discovered by each man. A good reference is *Fossil Feud* by Thom Holmes. Hint: the scientific names of organisms are often followed by the discoverer's last name.

Descent & Change Over Time 30

FO

Write the names of the creatures below in their correct geological eras.

trilobite   **allosaurus**   **dire wolf**
ammonite   **hadrosaur**   **armored fish**
woolly mammoth

Paleozoic: _____

_____

Mesozoic: _____

_____

Cenozoic: _____

_____

Humans in the Web of Life

Humans in the Web of Life 1

Human population growth has increased over the last 300 years. At the same time, the number of mammal and bird extinctions has also increased. List three reasons for this relationship.

A. _____

_____

B. _____

_____

C. _____

_____

Humans in the Web of Life 2

On your own paper, make a list of the clothes you are wearing today. How many different animals and plants were used to create your clothing? What were any plastics made from? Where might metals have been mined? Where would you look to find the answers to these questions?

Humans in the Web of Life 3

Sally is sick with food poisoning, caused by bacteria in undercooked food. Elwood has the flu, which is caused by a virus. Mark the following statements as true (T) or false (F).

____ A. Sally's illness is infectious.

____ B. Elwood's flu can be cured with antibiotics.

____ C. Seymour may have caught the flu by touching something Elwood touched.

____ D. Getting the flu will protect Elwood from food poisoning.

Humans in the Web of Life 4

On your own paper, make a list of what you ate yesterday. Put a check mark next to items grown within 10 miles of home, an X next to items grown somewhere in the United States, and an O next to items grown outside our country. How might your eating habits change if airplane traffic or delivery trucks were grounded for a week?

Humans in the Web of Life

Humans in the Web of Life 5   O

Parasites live at the expense of other organisms. **Symbionts** are two or more creatures that live together and benefit each other. **Commensals** live together, but don't have much interaction otherwise. Identify the relationship between humans and the following organisms.

A. *L. acidophilus* bacteria _____   B. Flu viruses _____

C. Head lice _____   D. Dogs _____

How might these relationships change over time? _____

_____

Humans in the Web of Life 6   A

Some estimates indicate that global warming could raise sea levels by 20 feet in the next 50 years. Answer the following questions on your own paper.

A. How would this affect the area where you now live?

B. How would rising temperatures and sea levels change where food is
    produced in the United States? Elsewhere in the world?

C. How might global warming affect the job you choose?

Humans in the Web of Life 7   A

A. What is the current population of the world? _____

B. What is the current population of the United States? _____

C. What was your source for the above answers? _____

_____

D. How does the population of your town or city affect the kinds of
    plants and animals that live near you? _____

_____

_____

Humans in the Web of Life

Humans in the Web of Life 8

A

On your own paper, write questions that have the following answers.

A. Pollution

B. Renewable resources

C. Fossil fuels

D. Biodiversity

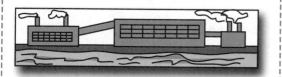

Humans in the Web of Life 9

A

What questions would you ask experts to determine whether the rise in average global temperature over the past 200 years may have been caused by the activities of humans?

_____

_____

_____

_____

_____

Humans in the Web of Life 10

U

Mice, mosquitoes, cockroaches, and other organisms thrive near humans in spite of efforts to destroy them. Humans encourage the growth of food organisms like corn, wheat, cows, and goats. Dogs, cats, and other pets provide companionship.

A. T or F: Humans consciously try to control which creatures live near them. _____

B. Examples of organisms used for food include _____ and _____.

Humans in the Web of Life 11

U

Physically, humans are typical mammals—they have a bony skeleton, hair, and nurse their young with milk. Behaviorally, humans have created a unique culture—a method for passing information from generation to generation through language.

A. T or F: Humans differ completely from other organisms. _____

B. Mammals possess a _____ skeleton, _____, and _____ their young.

Humans in the Web of Life

Humans in the Web of Life 12

U

In 1992, a freighter in the Pacific Ocean lost a cargo of 1,000 plastic bath toys. Seven months later, toys began washing up on beaches—some as far away as Maine and Scotland. Scientists are using the toys to learn about global ocean currents.

A. Scientists are using _____ to learn about ocean currents.

B. T or F: Water circulates between the Atlantic and Pacific Oceans. _____

Humans in the Web of Life 13

U

Water supplies contain traces of synthetic estrogens—biologically active hormones that might affect aquatic wildlife. Retaining water at sewage plants longer allows bacteria to break down the hormones more effectively into other compounds.

A. T or F: The affect of estrogens on aquatic organisms was proven to be harmful. _____

B. _____ break down estrogens, if given enough time.

Humans in the Web of Life 14

U

Carbon dioxide contributes to global warming by retaining heat, like the walls of a greenhouse. One possible solution is to pump excess carbon dioxide into deep ocean sediments where it will be trapped for a long time.

A. Carbon dioxide in the atmosphere retains _____.

B. T or F: No one has thought of a solution for global warming. _____

Humans in the Web of Life

Humans in the Web of Life 15

F

Unplowed grasslands are referred to by ecologists as "carbon sinks" because carbon is stored within the grass plants. Answer the following on your own paper.

A. In what forms is carbon stored?

B. Explain how carbon sinks can affect the amount of carbon dioxide in the air.

C. How might this affect overall temperatures worldwide?

Humans in the Web of Life 16

F

The air you exhale is approximately 78% nitrogen, 16% oxygen, and 4% carbon dioxide. The molecules of these gases constantly circulate in the atmosphere. You may share oxygen molecules once breathed by Julius Caesar or Beyoncé. On your

own paper, using at least six steps, show a possible pathway from one of these individuals to your lungs.

Humans in the Web of Life 17

F

Starlings are birds first introduced to Central Park in New York City by Eugene Scheifflin in 1890 and 1891. These birds rapidly expanded across the United States and have become so numerous they are often considered to be pests.

Why do populations of a species often become pests in new habitats? Explain your answer.

_____

_____

_____

Humans in the Web of Life 18

F

In the 1950s, the average fruiting season for mushrooms in England lasted 33 days. In the decade beginning in 2000, the fruiting season has increased to 75 days.

This (circle one):

A. Indicates that average global temperatures are decreasing.

B. Lends support to the idea that average global temperatures are rising.

C. Proves worldwide annual temperatures are permanently higher.

Humans in the Web of Life

Humans in the Web of Life 19

F

Between 10,000 to 15,000 years ago, mammoths, giant bears, ground sloths, and other large animals disappeared. During this same time period, humans are believed to have migrated to North America from Asia. This information allows us to say (circle one):

A. Human beings exterminated large animals in North America.

B. Climate change probably exterminated large animals.

C. Humans may have contributed to large animal extinctions.

D. Human migration probably had no effect on animal populations.

Humans in the Web of Life 20

D

As much as 25% of solid waste today is some form of plastic. On your own paper, make a list of all the objects in your class-room, as well as some of your personal items at home.

How many objects are plastic or have plastic parts? _____

How many of these items can be recycled? _____

How do you know? _____

_____

_____

Humans in the Web of Life 21

D

On your own paper, make a list of how you could conserve water…

A. in the kitchen,   B. in the bathroom,

C. at school, and   D. in the yard.

Calculate how much water your class could conserve per year if each person saved one gallon per toilet flush. (Placing a plastic 1-gallon water jug full of water with the cap on in the toilet's water tank can save a gallon of water per flush.)

_____

Humans in the Web of Life

Humans in the Web of Life 22

Plastic takes a long time to decompose naturally. Animals can mistake plastic for food or get tangled in items like plastic six-pack rings. On your own paper, devise a plan for using less plastic in your life and/or recycling the plastic you do use. Does your community have places to recycle plastic? If you don't know, how can you find out?

Humans in the Web of Life 23

It is estimated that every person in the United States uses 65 gallons of water per day. On your own paper, make a list of all the ways you use water. (It may help to think about how you use water in every room of your house and at school.)

Humans in the Web of Life 24

The three "Rs" of managing waste are "Reduce," "Reuse," and "Recycle." Americans throw out tons of aluminum each year, often in the form of aluminum cans. On your own paper, make a three-column list of ways you could reduce, reuse, and recycle aluminum cans.

Humans in the Web of Life 25

The metal mercury can be a major environmental pollutant. Answer the following questions on your own paper.

A. How is mercury harmful to living things?
B. Mercury often enters the atmosphere from coal-burning power plants. What factors in an ecosystem near a power plant would affect whether mercury concentrations became a concern?

Humans in the Web of Life

Humans in the Web of Life 26

A species of eastern European shrimp was found in the Great Lakes near Muskegon, Michigan. Answer the following questions on your own paper.

A. How did these shrimp most likely get there?
B. What are the dangers of such "foreign invaders" in a habitat new to them?

Humans in the Web of Life 27

In 1978, some fish with abnormal sexual organs containing a mixture of male and female tissue were found downstream  from a sewage treatment plant. Later, scientists determined that small concentrations of estrogen were causing the problems in the fish. Answer the following question on your own paper.

Why might estrogens cause these kinds of problems in fish?

Humans in the Web of Life 28

Who was Rachel Carson?

You can learn about her at <www.rachelcarson.org>.

Answer the following questions on your own paper.

A. What book made her famous?
B. What impact did she have on the development of pesticides and other chemicals?

Humans in the Web of Life 29

Answer the following questions on your own paper.

A. What is an organism's ecological niche?
B. What was the ecological niche of human beings before the invention of agriculture?
C. What is it now?

Math & Metrics in Life Science

Metric System Review & Conversion Tables

Our English system of weights and measures has a colorful history, including a length measurement called the foot based on the shoe size of a king and an inch defined as the length of three barleycorns placed end to end. But English measurements can be confusing and hard to convert into different units. Scientists use a **metric system** of weights and measures, called *Systeme International d'Unites* (SI for short), based on units of ten.

The basic unit of **length** is the **meter (m)**, which is slightly longer than the English yard. Prefixes are added to indicate measurements that increase or decrease by a factor of ten. So, a decimeter is 0.1 m, a centimeter is 0.01 m, and a millimeter is 0.001 m. To convert from one measurement to another, you just have to move a decimal point. If something measures 360 cm, calculate the number of meters by moving the decimal point two places to the left. 360 cm = 3.60 m.

Going in the other direction, one dekameter is 10 m, a hectometer is 100 meters, and a kilometer is 1,000 meters. 1 km = 0.6 miles. The same prefixes are used with all metric units.

The basic metric unit of **volume** is the **liter (L)**, approximately a quart. A liter is also equal to 1,000,000 mm³ (cubic millimeters). In addition, 1 L of water weighs 1 kg; 1 mL = 1,000 mm³ and weighs 1 gram. 1 cubic meter (m³) of water weighs 1 metric ton. 1 cubic centimeter is about the size of a sugar cube. Sometimes cubic centimeters (cm³) are referred to as "cc." 1 cm³ = 1 cc

Area is measured in **square meters** (m^2). 1 m^2 is approximately the surface area of a card table. **Mass** is measured in **grams** and **kilograms**. 1,000 kg = 1 metric ton, nearly the size of an English ton. **Force** is measured in **newtons** (N), with 1 newton being about a fifth of a pound.

Temperature is measured in **degrees Celsius** (°C), instead of degrees Fahrenheit (°F). The freezing point of water is 0°C and 32° F. °C = °F − 32 • 5/9; °F = (°C • 9/5) + 32

Some common conversions are listed below:

1 mm = 0.039 inch	1 inch = 2.54 cm
1 m = 3.281 feet	1 yard = 0.914 m
1 km = 0.621 miles	1 mile = 1.609 km
1 square meter = 10.764 square feet	1 square foot = 0.093 m^2
1 hectare = 2.471 acres	1 acre = 0.405 hectares
1 km^2 = 0.386 square mile	1 square mile = 2.59 km^2
1 m^3 = 1.31 cubic yards	1 cubic foot = 0.028 m^3
1 mL = 0.061 cubic inches	1 cubic inch = 16.387 cm^3
1 L = 1.057 quarts	1 quart = 0.946 L
1 g = 0.035 ounces	1 ounce = 28.35 g
1 kg = 2.204 pounds	1 pound = 0.454 kg
1 N (newton) = 0.2248 pounds	1 pound = 4.448 N

Math & Metrics in Life Science

Math & Metrics in Life Science 1 | M |

The largest flying insects ever known were dragonflies that lived during the Permian Period. One fossil has a wing that measures 280 millimeters (mm) long. Its total body length was 305 millimeters, and its wingspan (distance from wing tip to wing tip) was 686 millimeters. If 1 inch = 25.4 mm, what are these measurements in inches?

A. Wing length: 280 mm = _____ inches.

B. Body length: 305 mm = _____ inches.

C. Wingspan: 686 mm = _____ inches.

Math & Metrics in Life Science 2 | M |

At least 500 species of beneficial bacteria live in the human intestines. All together, they weigh about 3.3 pounds.

A. What is their weight in grams?

_____

B. How much do they weigh in kilograms? _____

C. If you weigh 54.4 kg and have 3.3 pounds of intestinal bacteria, what percentage of your body weight is intestinal bacteria? _____%

Math & Metrics in Life Science 3 | M |

Marvin ran into the classroom and said, "Help me! My friend, Oscar, has a temperature of 40° C." Assuming normal body temperature is 98.6° F, should you get ice cubes to cool Oscar down or blankets to warm him up? Explain your answer.

_____

_____

_____

_____

_____

Math & Metrics in Life Science

Math & Metrics in Life Science 4 [M]

The human stomach has a capacity of 1 to 1.6 liters.

A. What is the capacity range expressed in quarts?

_____ to _____ qts.

B. Would a half gallon jug hold your stomach contents? _____

The human bladder has a capacity of 600 to 800 mL.

C. What is the capacity range expressed in quarts?

_____ to _____ qts.

Math & Metrics in Life Science 5 [M]

An expedition of time travelers visited the Triassic Period and divided into two groups. One group encountered a species of dinosaur called Coelophysis that was 4 m from snout to tail. The other came across a male Herrerasaurus that was 15 feet long.

Which group found the largest

dinosaur? _____

_____

Math & Metrics in Life Science 6 [M]

Calculate the area of squares that are 1, 2, 3, 4, 5, and 6 cm on a side. Calculate the volume of cubes with the same dimensions. How does the rate of increase of area (in cm^2) compare to that of volume (in cm^3)? How does this difference affect the size to which an animal can grow? If the strength of support structures like legs are proportional to area, and animal weight is proportional to volume, why are monster spiders the size of houses impossible on Earth? Answer on your own paper.

Math & Metrics in Life Science 7 [M]

On a sheet of paper, create a square 20 cm on a side. On the back of that sheet of paper, make a list of all the plants or animals you can think of that would fit within  that square. Repeat the process twice more by making squares 2 cm and 2 mm on a side, respectively. Each of these squares is one-tenth the size of the one before it. Is it harder to think of animals and plants that fit in the smaller squares?

Math & Metrics in Life Science

Math & Metrics in Life Science 8   M

Scientists must use units called **microns** to measure the smallest life forms.
1 mm = 1,000 microns. Some of the smallest viruses are measured in
nanometers. 1 micron = 1,000 nm.
How many of each of the following organisms would fit end-to-end in a space
1 mm long?

A. *E. coli* bacterium 2.6 microns long   _____

B. Bacterial virus 200 nm long   _____

C. Influenza virus 100 nm in diameter   _____

D. Polio virus 5 nm in diameter   _____

Math & Metrics in Life Science 9   M

Scientific notation expresses very large or very small numbers as "powers of
ten." 1,000 can be expressed as 1×10^3 (or 1 x 10 x 10 x 10). 1/1,000 becomes
1×10^{-3}, which means 1/(10 x 10 x 10). The minus sign of the exponent indicates
you are dividing 1 by the product of tens.

Express the following numbers in scientific notation.

A. 10,000 _____   B. 100,000 _____

C. 1/1,000,000 _____   D. 1/100,000 _____

Math & Metrics in Life Science 10   M

Numbers in scientific notation can be translated to "normal" numbers by
moving the decimal point to the right of the first number by the number of
spaces indicated by the exponent if it is positive, and to the left if the exponent
is negative.

$$1.2 \times 10^2 = 1,200. \qquad 1.2 \times 10^{-2} = 0.012.$$

Convert the following.

A. 6.9×10^4 = _____   B. 7.1×10^{-3} = _____

C. 2.8×10^{-5} = _____   D. 9.5×10^7 = _____

Answer Keys

Diversity of Life
(Page 2)
1. Variable answers
2. A. FS   B. ES   C. BB   D. D
   E. ES   F. BB
3. A. 3, 6   B. 2, 3   C. 1, 4, 5
(Page 3)
4. A. I   B. S
   C. N (Crustacean)   D. S   E. I
   F. I   G. S   H. I
5. Seeds have a food source for the developing plant embryo; spores do not. Variable drawings.
6. 1. C   2. A
7. Variable answers.
   A. Biomes are environments with similar climates and ecological communities.
   B. Estuaries are where fresh and salt water mix.
   C. A deciduous forest is made up of trees that annually shed their leaves.
   D. Grasses are the dominant community plant in grasslands. Annual rainfall is between 25 cm and 75 cm in grasslands.
(Page 4)
8. 1. D   2. B   3. E
9. Experiments are designed to result in a "yes" or "no" answer to a scientific question.
10. A. What kind of teeth does it have? Is it built for offense or defense?
   B. What is the nature of the surrounding sediment? What other animals and plants are found with it?
   C. How does its skeletal structure compare to modern animals' known characteristics?
(Page 5)
11. A. animals   B. cell   C. fresh, salt
12. A. teosinte   B. T
13. A. large eyes, flying skills   B. F
14. A. half   B. T
(Page 6)
15. A. poor, half   B. trees
16. A. Coleoptera
   B. angiosperm (Anthophyta)

C. Pan
D. Animalia, Vertebrata, Mammalia, Primate, Hominidae, *Homo, sapiens*
17. A. Plantae   B. Protista
   C. Animalia
   D. Fungi   E. Monera
18. A. spider   B. birds   C. a bee
   D. Variable answers
(Page 7)
19. It might attract fly pollinators (among other possibilities); Could mask odor and see if plant gets as effectively pollinated.
20. A lichen
22. Careful observation allows you to see important details for identification.
(Page 8)
26. Variety, distinctness, or separateness of being; Biodiversity provides the raw material to meet an ecosystem's needs when change occurs.
(Page 9)
27. Variable answers
28. There are more beetles than all other animal species combined.
29. Ascomycetes: *Aspergillus*, pink bread mold
Basidiomycetes: mushroom, "toadstools"
Zygomycetes: black bread mold, dung mold
Each group of fungi makes its spores in a different way.

Energy Flow in Living Communities
(Page 10)
1. Producers (base): D. grass, E. sagebrush
First-order consumers (middle): B. prairie dog, C. grasshopper, G. buffalo
Second-order consumers (top): A. hawk, F. coyote
2. Variable answers, but nearly all will depend on the sun. Hydroelectric, wind, and solar power can be replenished; fossil fuels cannot.
3. Producers: wheat, tomatoes, pineapple, oregano, olives, etc.
Consumers: cows, pigs, seafood, humans, etc.

(Page 11)

4. Variable answers

5. Without decomposers, the rest of the ecosystem would collapse from lack of resources.

6. What are the major gases in the atmosphere? Are they in chemical equilibrium? Is there free oxygen? (Reactive gases like oxygen have to be resupplied by living things.)

7. A. What is water loss through plant leaves called?
   B. What is liquid or frozen water that falls from clouds?
   C. What are oil and gas?
   D. What is the process of breaking down carbon compounds into CO_2 and water?

(Page 12)

8. 1. D   2. C   3. B

9. A. $6CO_2 + 6H_2O \rightarrow C_6H_{12}O_6 + 6 O_2$
   B. $C_6H_{12}O_6 + 6 O_2 \rightarrow 6CO_2 + 6H_2O +$ energy (ATP)
   C. The formulas are the reverse of each other with different forms of energy involved.

10. A. Metaphase B. Anaphase
    C. Prophase
    D. Mitosis produces two cells with the same number of chromosomes while meiosis yields four cells with half the chromosomes of the parent cell.

11. A. F   B. T

(Page 13)

12. A. oxygen
    B. No. No photosynthesis would occur, so no oxygen would be produced.

13. A. adenosine triphosphate   B. T

14. A. mitochondria   B. bacteria
    C. energy

15. A. oxygen   B. not expect

(Page 14)

16. Energy is lost at each step in the food chain.
    A. mosasaur
    B. alga (a producer or plant)

17. Adenosine triphosphate (ATP)

18. 1. E   2. D   3. B   4. A

(Page 15)

19. Methane is a by-product of decomposition. Methane is produced by other natural processes.

20. C. Oil is a limited resource.

(Page 16)

25. A. Green plants form the base of the food chain. They are primary producers of food energy.
    B. All levels above the base level have consumers.
    C. The base level contains most of the sun's energy.
    D. Decomposers return raw materials to the soil and air for use by plants.

26. Mayfly larva H, Stonefly nymph H, Caddisfly nymph O, Dragonfly adult C, Dragonfly nymph C.
    Variable answers.

(Page 17)

27. It's a buffer against combustion (because of the oxygen present) and helps prevent certain breathing problems. Materials, shielding, energy, gravity, food, and inputs/outputs are also mentioned.

28. At least some eggs will survive to become adults; web sites, encyclopedias, insect guides

29. A. An enzyme is an organic catalyst.
    B. A catalyst promotes chemical reactions.
    C. A carbohydrate has the chemical group COOH.
    D. Ribosomal RNA forms the structure of ribosomes.

30. Cheetahs, jaguars, and short-faced bears were the fastest runners as evidenced by their body anatomy

Organization of the Human Body
(Page 18)

1. Pulse will be higher standing than sitting and higher running than standing. Pulse results from the beating of your heart.

2. The second person must observe you drop the paper, then react. This takes longer than getting "release" and "catch" impulses from the same brain.

3. Incisors cut and shear like scissors. Canines puncture and tear. Molars crush food.

4. By focusing at a distance, the images from right and left eyes don't merge completely, but partially overlap instead.

(Page 19)

5. The right forearm feels cooler because the alcohol evaporates faster, carrying more heat away. Alcohol baths were used to reduce fevers.

6. A. Immune system
   B. Respiratory system
   C. Digestive system
   D. Skeletal system

7. A. What are the four major human blood groups/types?
   B. What blood cells play a role in the defense of the body?
   C. Which chambers of the heart pump blood?

(Page 20)

8. 1. E/C/D 2. D 3. C

9. Variable answers.
   A. What increases metabolic rate while maintaining calcium and potassium levels in the blood?
   B. What master gland regulates all the other glands?
   C. What elevates heart rate, blood pressure, blood sugar, and breathing, but suppresses digestion?
   D. What gland regulates the immune system?

10. Variable responses.

(Page 21)

11. A. F   B. viruses, bacteria, fungi, insects
12. A. T   B. contract
13. A. stroke   B. aneurysm
14. A. red cells, white cells, platelets
    B. 10%

(Page 22)

15. A. cerebrum, cerebellum, medulla
    B. central nervous system
16. A. Interneurons connect sensory & motor neurons.
    B. Motor neurons innervate muscles.
    C. Sensory neurons transmit signals from receptors.
    D. Effectors carry out CNS commands.
    E. Spinal cord is the main nerve trunk line.
17. A. NI   B. NI   C. I   D. I
    E. NI

(Page 23)

18. A nephron
19. Variable answers
20. You will be more susceptible to infection, will show a low white blood cell count, and have a weakened immune system.

(Page 24)

22. There are no sensors in the blind spot where the optic nerve meets the retina.
23. A. Percentages will vary.
    B. Free-hanging earlobes
24. Your brain receives input from both thumb and forefinger. Since your partner's finger blocks normal input from your finger, your brain misinterprets the message.

(Page 25)

25. Best score for C because the combined words have meaning. If you can make a sentence from key words or letters in a list, the list is easier to remember.
26. Problem with blood clotting
27. A. Estrogen produces female secondary sexual characteristics, like breasts.
    B. Progesterone promotes the growth of the uterine lining.
    C. Testosterone produces male secondary sexual characteristics, like facial hair.

(Page 26)

28. A. Active immunity: The body creates antibodies in response to a disease organism.
    Passive: Protection by antibodies produced by the mother in the womb or by vaccine injection
    B. Finding and destroying harmful bacteria and viruses.
29. A. the liver   B. a virus
    C. It saves lives, increases productivity, and decreases misery of people.
30. Prions are protein fragments, not complete organisms. Prions form tangles and holes in brain tissue.

Life Cycles of Organisms
(Page 27)

1. A. T   B. F
2. The ladybug has complete metamorphosis with four distinct stages: egg, larva, pupa, and adult.

3. The endosperm provides food for the growing seedling.

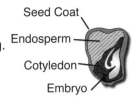

Seed Coat
Endosperm
Cotyledon
Embryo

4. The axolotl lives in the water, as evidenced by gills and a fish-like tail.

(Page 28)
5. A. 1 & 2   B. 3   C. 3 & 4   D. 2
6. A. Dicot   B. Angiosperm   C. Pollen
   D. Beneath the petals
7. 1. E   2. D   3. C   4. B

(Page 29)
8. A. What kind of life cycle does a fern or moss have?
   B. What stage of a fern produces gametes?
   C. What is an adult, spore-producing fern called?
   D. What structure holds spores?
9. The different life stages can eat different foods. You could observe and document the reproductive success of insects with incomplete and complete metamorphosis in the same environment.
10. Sphinx riddle: a human crawls as a baby, walks on two legs when mature, and needs a cane when old. What crawls in the morning, sleeps at noon, and flies at night?
11. A. protection, water conservation
    B. brood pouches

(Page 30)
12. A. lacewings   B. help
13. A. chemical signal   B. spores
14. A. T   B. potato plants
15. A. malaria, yellow fever
    B. food, reproduce

(Page 31)
16. A. in blood banks
    B. They jump you.
    C. It gets hopping mad.
17. A. Stages: D, B, A, C   B. frog
18. Repellents would have to "turn off" genes or be able to act on individuals with active genes.
19. A. on anthers   B. in the pistil
    C. creates a pathway for sperm to reach the egg cell
    D. top of stem beneath the petals

(Page 32)
20. 1. b   2. d   3. e   4. a   5. c
22. Growth rate may be affected by temperature, amount of food, humidity, and other factors.

(Page 33)
23. In general, adults tend to prefer the dark, and larvae show no strong preference.
24. Adults tend to prefer the cool end of the tray. The more beetles you test, the more confident you can be of results.
25. Since these beetles eat grain, farmers would like to know how to prevent that!

(Page 34)
29. Carnivorous plants eat animals to acquire minerals and other dietary requirements missing in their environment.

Descent & Change Over Time
(Page 35)
1. An adult is about 3.5 times the size of an infant. A baby's head is about one-fourth of his total length, whereas an adult is 7 or 8 "heads" tall.
2. The black moths will survive better on dark trunks because they are harder to see. The frequency of dark moths will increase.
3. Birds are believed to be the living descendents of *T. rex* and other theropod dinosaurs.

(Page 36)
4. Horse legs have lengthened and the number of toes has decreased.
5. A. F   B. T   C. F
6. 1. D   2. A   3. C
7. Plates should be thin and porous with an indication of holes for blood vessels.

(Page 37)
8. 1. C, because it is lower in the strata
   2. a dike
   3. The strata slipped past each other.
9. A. What other fossils are with it? What geological formation is it in?
   B. What kind of teeth does it have? Were stomach contents preserved? Are there associated plant fossils?
   C. What does it look like? How does its structure compare to modern animals?
10. A. 50%   B. 0%

(Page 38)
11. A. United States
    B. Thomas Jefferson, mastodons
12. A. the Gobi Desert/Mongolia
    B. F
13. A. different   B. disasters
(Page 39)
14. A. hip, leg   B. F
15. A. T   B. resistant
16. Yellowstone Lake was originally connected to neighboring lakes. Over time, genetic drift and new selection pressures changed the population in Yellowstone Lake.
17. More people who were tolerant of lactose survived and passed their genes on. Natural selection.
(Page 40)
18. Smaller animals eat less, can have larger populations, and won't suffer if natural predators are absent.
19. Horns could be for defense, sexual selection, warning communication, or perhaps involved in breathing. Are the ornaments limited to one sex? Is their form consistent with any proposed function?
20. 1. B 2. C 3. D 4. A
(Page 41)
21. Water erosion may have moved the fossil to a new location.
22. A. 4.1 feet   B. 16.4 feet
23. Die under water or get buried fast in a place that stays undisturbed over geologic time scales
(Page 42)
24. Minerals become crystallized in the pores of bones.
25. Like geological strata, the older materials are at the "bottom of the heap." Variable conclusions.
26. A. fossil resin
    B. various arthropods and the occasional vertebrate
    C. fragmented, incomplete, or degraded DNA.
       DNA could also be mixed with that of other creatures.
27. Ornithomimus

(Page 43)
28. A. Their entire species dies off.
    B. If their cold-adapted habitat on mountains disappears, they have nowhere to go.
29. Variable answers
30. Paleozoic: trilobite, armored fish
    Mesozoic: allosaurus, hadrosaur, ammonite
    Cenozoic: woolly mammoth, dire wolf

Humans in the Web of Life
(Page 44)
 1. Loss of habitat, killing for food or pleasure, death through pollution, climate and/or habitat change
 2. Variable list of clothes. Plastics are made from hydrocarbons. Encyclopedias and web search engines can provide basic information.
 3. A. F   B. F   C. T   D. F
 4. Variable responses, but a large part of food from grocery chains comes from non-local sources.
(Page 45)
 5. A. Symbiont   B. Parasite
    C. Parasite
    D. Symbiont or Commensal
    Answers will vary. Relationships could change if the host of a parasite dies, or the environment in which a relationship takes place changes.
 6. A. Variable answers
    B. Productive farmland will follow moisture and temperature shifts. Lowland areas will flood.
    C. Variable answers
 7. Variable answers
(Page 46)
 8. Variable answers
 9. Variable answers. How are human population growth and activities affecting greenhouse gas concentrations?
10. A. T
    B. cows, corn (also wheat and goats)
11. A. F   B. bony, hair, nurse
(Page 47)
12. A. plastic bath toys   B. T
13. A. F   B. Bacteria
14. A. heat   B. F

(Page 48)
15. A. As sugars, cell walls, and other organic compounds
    B. Carbon sinks lower atmospheric CO_2.
    C. This would reduce global temperatures.
16. Variable answers, but could include plants, animals, in the air, and combined with minerals.
17. They have no natural enemies and may crowd out native species in a similar ecological niche.
18. B

(Page 49)
19. C
20. The recycle symbol with the enclosed number lets you know how easily it can be recycled.
21. Fix leaks, use more water-efficient devices, add a brick to toilet tank, turn off water during toothbrushing, use soaker hose instead of sprinkler, etc. If each person saves 5 gallons/day, that equals 1,825 gallons/person/year.

(Page 50)
22. Check with your town landfill or waste-disposal company.
23. Answers will vary.
24. Answers will vary.
25. A. Mercury causes nerve and brain damage, especially in the young.
    B. Topography of surrounding land, air currents, and rainfall patterns would affect concentrations.

(Page 51)
26. A. As ballast in ships
    B. They can spread and displace native species and may be hard to control.
27. Estrogens are female hormones that affect sexual characteristics and development.
28. A. *Silent Spring*
    B. Her research caused the reduction in some pesticide use and raised awareness of harm caused by chemicals.
29. A. Their "job" in the ecosystem
    B. Omnivores and top-level predators
    C. Keystone species worldwide

Math & Metrics in Life Science
(Page 53)
1. A. 280 mm = 11 inches
   B. 305 mm = 12 inches
   C. 686 mm = 27 inches
2. A. 3.3 pounds = 1,500 g
   B. 1.5 kg
   C. 2.8%
3. Ice to cool him down because $40°\ C = 104°\ F$

(Page 54)
4. A. 1.1 to 1.7 quarts
   B. yes
   C. 0.63 to 0.85 quarts
5. Herrerasaurus is bigger by about two feet.
6. Areas in cm^2: 1, 4, 9, 16, 25, 36
   Volumes in cm^3: 1, 8, 27, 64, 125, 216;
   Weight limits maximum growth and outstrips ability of legs to support it.
7. Yes, we tend to recognize creatures within our size range.

(Page 55)
8. A. 385   B. 5,000
   C. 10,000   D. 200,000
9. A. 1×10^4 B. 1×10^5
   C. 1×10^{-6} D. 1×10^{-5}
10. A. 69,000   B. 0.0071
    C. 0.000028   D. 95,000,000

Teacher Resources

Bourne, Barbara, Editor. *Taking Inquiry Outdoors.* York, Maine: Stenhouse Publishers, 2000.

Carmazine, Scott. *The Naturalist's Year.* New York: John Wiley & Sons, Inc., 1987.

Carson, Rachel. *Silent Spring.* Boston: Houghton Mifflin Company, 1962.

Cornell, Joseph. *Sharing Nature with Children.* Nevada City, CA: Dawn Publications, 1998.

Dashefsky, H. Steven. *Kids Can Make a Difference! Environmental Science Activities.* New York: TAB Books, Division of McGraw-Hill Inc., 1995.

Dunn, Gary A. *Project B.U.G.S.* (*Better Understanding of the Great Six-Leggers).* Lansing, Michigan: Young Entomologists Society, 1994.

Garber, Steven. *The Urban Naturalist.* New York: John Wiley & Sons, Inc., 1987.

Gardner, Martin. *Entertaining Science Experiments with Everyday Objects.* New York: Dover Publications, Inc., 1981.

Holmes, Thom. *Fossil Feud.* New Jersey: Julian Messner, 1991.

Johnson, Jinny. (Elizabeth Gray, illustrator) *An Inside Look at Animals.* New York: Reader's Digest Kids, 1994.

Kneidel, Sally Stenhouse. *Creepy Crawlies and the Scientific Method.* Golden, CO: Fulcrum Publishing, 1993.

Raham, R. Gary. *Dinosaurs in the Garden.* New Jersey: Plexus Publications, 1988.

Raham, R. Gary. *Explorations in Backyard Biology, Drawing on Nature in the Classroom, Grades 4-6.* Portsmouth, NH: Teacher Ideas Press, 1996.

Raham, R. Gary. *The Deep Time Diaries.* Golden, CO: Fulcrum Publishing, 2000.

Raham, R. Gary. *Science Tutor: Life Science.* Mark Twain Media, Inc., Publishers, 2005.

Robertson, Matthew (Ed.). *The Big Book of Bugs.* New York: Welcom, 1999.

VanCleave, Janice. *Biology for Every Kid.* New York: John Wiley & Sons, Inc., 1990.